DESTROYING

DESTRUCTIVE
Prophecy

Dr Daniel Olukoya

Destroying Destructive Prophecy

By

Dr Daniel Olukoya

Destroying Destructive Prophecy
©2010.Dr Daniel Olukoya

A publication of
MOUNTAIN OF FIRE AND MIRACLES MINISTRIES
13, Olasimbo Street, off Olumo Road, Onike,
P. O. Box 2990, Sabo, Yaba, Lagos, Nigeria.

ISBN: 978-978-8424-56-7

For further information or permission, contact:
Email: pasteurdanielolukoya_french@yahoo.fr
            mfmhqworldwide@mountainoffire.org

Or visit our website: www.mountainoffire.org
http://mfmbiligualbooks4evangelism.blogspot.com/

Prophecy is history in advance. It is foretelling or prediction. There are good and evil prophecies. There are harmless prophecies and there are harmful prophecies.

In this book, we shall be looking at the topic titled, "Destroying Destructive Prophecy."

1 Samuel 17:41 says, *"And the Philistine came and drew near unto David; and the man that bare the shield went before him."*

Goliath challenged the people of Israel twice per day for forty days. He came eighty times saying, "Bring a man to come and fight me. Bring your champion. If I defeat him, you become our slaves but if he defeats me, we become your slaves." God was watching him all these eighty times as if He did not hear what he was saying. Goliath had the armies of Israel beaten hands down. We know the true soldiers when giants come to battle. David was not impressed with Goliath at all. He said, "Who is this man? How can this fellow defy the armies of God?" By the eighty-fourth time that Goliath came, David was ready for him. Without a Goliath, there is no David. It was Goliath that really produced David. When David dealt with Goliath, he became somebody to be reckoned with. I Samuel 17:41-43 says, "And the Philistine came on and drew near unto David; and the man that bares the shield went before him. And when the Philistine looked about, and saw David, he disdained him; for he was but a youth, and ruddy, and of a fair countenance. And the Philistine said unto David, Am I a dog that thou comest to me with staves? And the philistine cursed David by his gods." Why did he do that? He did it in order to defeat David. He called for demonic assistance. Verse 44 says, *"And the Philistine said to David, Come to me, and I will give thy flesh unto the fowls of the. air, and to the beasts of the field."* The destructive prophecy made against David started here. Verse 45: "Then said David to the Philistine, Thou comest to me with a sword, and with a spear, and with a shield: but I come to thee in the name of the Lord of hosts, the God of the armies of Israel, whom thou hast defied."

In the foregoing, David started his counter prophecy. So, when somebody pronounces a vindictive prophecy against you, what you need to do is to utter a counter prophecy.

When two prophecies confront each other, the one that is backed by the power of God will defeat the one that is backed by evil powers. David continued his prophecy against Goliath: Verses 46 -47 *"This day will the Lord deliver thee into mine hand; and I will smite thee, and take thine head from thee: and I will give the carcases of the host of the Philistines this day unto the fowls of the air, and to the wild beasts of the earth; that all the earth may know that there is a God in Israel. And all this assembly shall know that the Lord saveth not with sword and spear; for the battle is the Lord's, and he will give you into our hands"* - a counter prophecy. Fortunately, Goliath had a very big head, so the stones of David had no problem locating it. And immediately Goliath was brought down, the armies of the Philistines fled. That is always the pattern; immediately the strongman in charge of your case is brought down, all the small ones supporting him will scatter.

WHAT IS PROPHECY?

Prophecy is history in advance. It is foretelling or prediction. There are good and evil prophecies. There are harmless prophecies and there are harmful prophecies. Just as we have good prayers, we also have satanic prayers. There are verbal prophecies, mental prophecies, silent prophecies and loud prophecies. There are good and evil wishes, that is; somebody can wish you well or evil. Silent evil prophecies are real problems because the perpetrator is unknown. He or she is silently prophesying against another person while smiling.

WHAT CONSTITUTES EVIL AND DESTRUCTIVE PROPHECIES?

1. Horizontal curses: These are curses between men. They are destructive prophecies issued against people.

2. Clinical prophecy: There are satanic clinical prophecies issued by doctors upon people's lives. I want you to know that a doctor can see what the devil wants him to see. A doctor can tell a person that he has a condition which the person does not have. And immediately the person begins to think

about it, he will begin to have it. I read a story of someone that went for a laboratory test and was mistakenly given a medical result of someone else. The result stated that he had HIV. And his own result that was devoid of HIV was given to another person. The man with the HIV positive result called the whole family told them what happened and assured them that he was not going to die alone. He woke up that night and poisoned the food meant for the family. He killed himself and everybody, only for the laboratory attendant to rush to his house the following day to say that they were sorry for giving him the wrong result.

3. Incantations.
4. Spell: Someone upon whom a spell has been cast will do the wrong things.
5. Hypnotism: It is the weapon commonly used by kidnappers whereby they prophesy to people in order to make them fools.
6. Evil wishes.
7. Satanic prayers: So many people are praying such prayers now. Some wicked debtors pray satanic prayers against their creditors. A fornicator did not

pray to the Lord to deliver her from the spirit of fornication, but when she got pregnant, she laid her hand on her stomach and prayed that the pregnancy should be aborted. What she needed to do was to command fornication to get out of her life. It is a satanic prayer.

8. Consultation with satanic prophets: Any rich person who uses his money to sponsor someone who tells him that God says he will sponsor his church building and send his children to school is putting his money under a curse. Do not use your money to sponsor rebellion, because it will put your wealth under a curse. Do not think that it is everyone that comes to church that wants to go to heaven. Some people are in church only to buy and sell. They believe there is market where there is a multitude of people. Some people come to look for beautiful ladies who will respect them because they are tired of the ladies of the world. Some come to steal from people, just like the Bible says that the house of God is like a net thrown into the sea. The net will catch various kinds of fishes, and it is the duty of the word of God to bring out the good ones among them. Some people are not interested in prayers and

sermons. They only wait for the service to close and they begin to announce what they have to sell. It is not everyone that comes to church that wants to go to heaven. There are agents of darkness as well as witches in all the churches. Some hang their powers outside before they come in, and collect them on their way out. Some people come to the service to spot those who they believe have problems, and lure them to satanic places where they siphon their money and virtues. Be very careful where you go for solution. Consulting satanic prophets brings destructive prophecy upon your life.

9. Self-imposed curses: When you curse yourself, you are issuing an evil prophecy against your own life. When you make statements such as "My headache, my migraine, my chest pain, my poor leg etc, you allot evil to yourself. It is a package of the enemy. When you say something is yours, it becomes yours.

10. Fortune telling.

11. Astrology.

12. Horoscope.

13. Any means apart from the Holy Ghost to know the future: The enemy can manipulate it.

14. Silent evil wishes backed up by evil spiritual powers: There are people who can stand on the highway and all they need to do for an accident to happen is to wish that it happens. And before you know it, it is done. You may find this hard to believe but it is true.

15. Envious expectation: They are people who are envious of others and are waiting for the day they will fall. They are envious of your marriage and waiting for the day your husband will kick you out.

16. Inner murdering spirit: The Bible calls anyone that hates his brother a murderer. Some people are armed robbers inside. They are wielding cutlasses there to cut. The only problem is that they cannot do the cutting physically. They have an inner murdering spirit.

17. Satanic letters: There are some people who write satanic letters and circulate them to people and tell them to circulate the same letters to ten or twenty persons. And if they do not, something evil will happen. If you make the mistake of circulating them as they said, you sign their package.

18. Praise name.
19. The prayer of a sinner on your behalf.
20. Mimicking evil songs: There are many evil songs around now. If you sing with them, you get into trouble.
21. Witchcraft decisions.
22. Direct satanic prophecy.

WHY ARE THESE PROPHECIES DANGEROUS?

They are dangerous because words have destructive powers. Words can travel from generation to generation. An evil prophecy has the power to redirect your destiny. It has potent controlling powers to manipulate a person's life. These evil prophecies have what is called a shadowing power. This is the reason why David did not keep quiet when Goliath spoke. He replied immediately and said, "*I come against you, in the name of the Lord of host. Today, you too will die.*"

Sometime ago, a certain sister came to me crying. She followed her friend to see a certain prophet, who told her that she would die. I told her to go back and tell the prophet that her pastor said it was he the prophet who would die and not her. She was hesitant but I persuaded her and she did it. Within seven days, that prophet was dead. If she had accepted it, she would have gone. Some people have collected evil prophecies when they were ignorant of these things. Some have allowed witches to lay hands on their heads during their engagement or marriage ceremonies. And many babies have been cuddled by the hands of people possessed with marine powers on the day of their dedication and destructive prophecies were issued upon their lives. Normally when a person surrenders his life to Jesus, receives the baptism of the Holy Spirit, and begins to grow in his walk with the Lord; some things will disappear from his life without him praying particularly about those things. Therefore, it is very important to get serious with the Lord.

WHY DESTRUCTIVE PROPHECIES FLOURISH IN THE LIVES OF CHRISTIANS

Hebrews 5:12-14 explains why destructive prophecies flourish in the lives of Christians. It says, "For when for the time ye ought to be teachers, ye have need that one teach you again which be the first principles of the oracles of God, and are become such as have need of milk, and not of strong meat. For every one that useth milk is unskillful in the word of righteousness: for he is a babe. But strong meat belongeth to them that are of full age, even those who by reason of use have their senses exercised to discern both good and evil. The prosperity of destructive prophecies is due to the fact that many churchgoers are babies. Kidnappers are able to slap born-again Christians and they will get confused because they are babies. Many who claim that they are growing are not really growing, they are just getting fat. There is no change in the quality of their holiness, prayers and Bible reading. They remain in the same level for years. Lack of spiritual growth opens up people's lives to attacks.

HOW TO DEAL WITH DESTRUCTIVE PROPHECIES

1. Repent of any known sin and stop issuing curses on yourself.

2. Constantly charge yourself with the fire of God. You could sit down for thirty minutes and pray this prayer point: "I charge my body with the fire of God, in Jesus' name."

3. Bind every evil word targeted at you.

4. Reverse evil prophecies.

5. Command the stubborn destructive prophecies to backfire.

6. Destroy their effects and consequences.

7. Barricade your life from further attacks.

I want you to know that there are powers and personalities that are not happy as you move about doing your own things. That is what is known as the battles of life. All playful curses that your parents, friends and others are issuing against you are destructive prophecies and you must deal with them. However, if you have not surrendered your life to Christ, you will not be able to deal thoroughly with destructive prophecies. To destroy them totally, you need to give your life to Christ. If you are ready to do so, make the following confessions: "Lord Jesus, I come before you today. I surrender my life to you. I know that I am a sinner. Forgive me and wash me with your precious blood. Take absolute control of my life. Thank you Lord Jesus, in Jesus' name. Amen.

Beloved, please take the prayer points below aggressively because the issue at hand is a very serious one.

PRAYER POINTS

1. Every hanging power waiting to attack my blessings, destroy your owners, in the name of Jesus.
2. Every hanging power in my house contrary to my destiny, die, in the name of Jesus.
3. Every incantation issued against my career, backfire, in the name of Jesus.
4. Thou curse of Goliath of my father's house, die, in the name of Jesus.
5. Thou curse of Goliath of my mother's house, die, in the name of Jesus.
6. Thou curse of limitations in my father's house, die, in the name of Jesus.
7. Thou curse of limitations in my mother's house, die, in the name of Jesus.
8. Thou power of destructive prophecy, die, in the name of Jesus.
9. My life, become too hot for witchcraft powers, in the name of Jesus.
10. Every witchcraft power assigned against me, go back to your sender, in the name of Jesus.
11. Oh ground, become burning fire to every stubborn witchcraft power, in the name of Jesus.
12. Every witchcraft Pharaoh pursuing my destiny, what are you waiting for? Die, in the name of Jesus.

ABOUT D. K. OLUKOYA

Dr. D. K. Olukoya is the General Overseer of the Mountain of Fire and Miracles Ministries and the Battle Cry Ministries. He holds a First Class Honours Degree in Microbiology from the University of Lagos, Nigeria and a Ph.D. in Molecular Genetics from the University of Reading, United Kingdom. As a researcher, he has over eighty scientific publications to his credit. Anointed by God, Dr. Olukoya is a teacher, prophet, evangelist and preacher of the word. His life and that of his wife, Shade and their son, Elijah Toluwani, are living proofs that all power belongs to God.

ABOUT MOUNTAIN OF FIRE AND MIRACLES MINISTRIES

Mountain of Fire and Miracles Ministries, is a ministry devoted to the revival of apostolic signs, Holy Ghost fireworks and the unlimited demonstration of the power of God to deliver to the uttermost. Absolute holiness within and without, as the greatest spiritual insecticide, and a condition for heaven is taught openly. MFM is a do-it-yourself Gospel Ministry, where your hands are trained to wage war and your fingers to fight.

A brief history of Mountain of Fire and Miracles Ministries Incorporated
The Mountain of Fire and Miracles was founded in 1989. The first meeting was held at the home of Dr. D. K Olukoya and had 24 persons in attendance. The Church later moved to No. 60, Old Yaba Road, Lagos, and then to the present International Headquarters, site on 24th April, 1994. The Mountain of Fire and Miracles Ministries' Headquarters is the largest single Christian congregation in Africa, with attendance of over

---

200,000 in single meetings. Mountain of Fire and Miracles Ministries is a full gospel ministry devoted to the revival of apostolic signs, Holy Ghost fireworks and the unlimited demonstration of the power of God to deliver to the uttermost. Absolute holiness, within and without, as the greatest spiritual insecticide and a pre-requisite for heaven is taught openly. MFM is a do-it-yourself Gospel ministry, where your hands are trained to wage war and your fingers to do battle.

YORUBA PUBLICATIONS

FRENCH PUBLICATIONS

ANNUAL 70 DAYS PRAYER AND FASTING PUBLICATIONS